Buil

By Nick Rebman

SPARKS

Picture Glossary

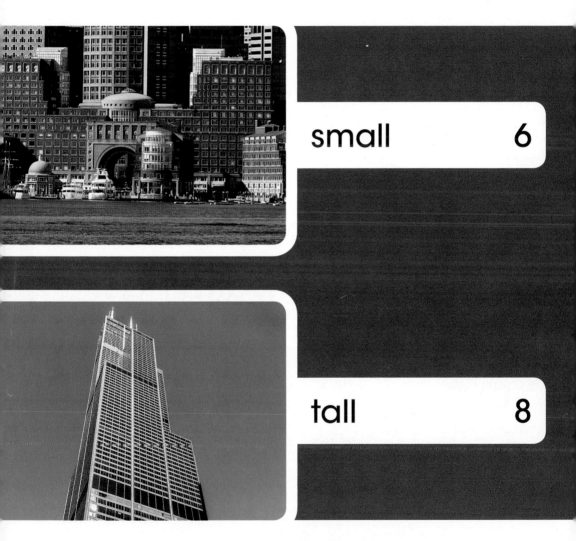

small   6

tall   8

Mills Haven School

3

I am in the city.

I see many buildings.

buildings

Some buildings are small.

This is a small building.

Some buildings are tall.

This is a very tall building.

tall

I want to go to the top.

This is what I see at the top of the building.

top

I look outside.

I can see many
buildings and lights.

lights

I am in the city.

I see many small and tall buildings.

city

Do You Know?

What do you see?

buildings

city

lights

top